RACING CARS

SEVENTY YEARS OF RECORD BREAKING

With an introduction by Ferruccio Bernabò

CRESCENT BOOKS

Contents

Acknowledgments for photographs used in this book:

Alfa Romeo: 100, 101
Ferruccio Bernabo: pages 5, 7, 8, 9, 11; 2-4, 6, 7, 9, 11, 13, 14, 17-24, 29, 32, 44, 45
Foto Bertazzini: 27
C. Bevilacqua: 65-96, 99, 103
S. Boroli: 97, 98, 102
Camera Press: 108
C. Dani: 1, 8, 10, 12, 25, 26, 28, 31, 33, 34, 53
Farabola: page 64
IGDA: page 10, 30, 35-43, 55, 57
G. Mairani: 62
Mercedes: 5, 15, 16
Montagu Motor Museum: pages 4, 6
Motor Sport: 106, 107, 111, page 64
Motoring News & Features: 109, 110, 112
Publifoto: 104, page 64
F. Villani: 46-52,.54, 56, 58-61, 63, 64, page 64

Translated from the Italian of Ferruccio Bernabò

© Istituto Geografico De Agostini, Novara 1969
English Edition © Orbis Publishing Limited, London 1971
Printed in Italy by IGDA, Novara
Library of Congress catalog card number 72-93844

Racing cars are the most superb examples of the car builder's craft and the races for which they are made form one of the most exciting spectacles known to the public. They serve not only as publicity for the manufacturers, but as a testing ground for the complicated research and work that go into the building and perfecting of a car. To begin with, racing was absolutely necessary to the car builders as this was their only practical means of testing their progress. Today the situation has radically changed: manufacturers now concentrate on getting good competition results, but if this ultimately benefits production line cars it is almost incidental. This means that whereas earlier manufacturers needed racing, today its usefulness is relative, and it is now a highly specialised undertaking of interest to a relatively limited number of technicians.

Like all sports in which man takes great risks, racing driving contains a high element of drama and is a continual source of controversy. The defenders of motor racing maintain that all production cars would be twenty years behind were it not for those whose days are dedicated to the constant perfecting of the formulae, and the drivers who risk their lives. They claim that a victory is of far greater value to manufacturers, and even to the country the car represents, than any publicity campaign. The opponents of these theories wish the manufacturers to concentrate instead on new developments in cars more similar to those available to the public, and to improve their production by increasing quality, value and commercial organisation.

It is difficult for the public to take sides in this controversy. It would be nonsense to say that racing is totally useless. Many dependent industries (suppliers of tires, carburetors, lubricants, superchargers, electric circuits, brakes and gears, etc.) provide builders of racing cars with materials for technical as well as commercial reasons, hoping that the results of laboratory and experimental tests will be confirmed, or at least that they will find useful pointers for future research.

Obviously the point of these activities has decreased with time. The stimulating function of sporting technology no longer has the same importance as at the beginning of the century. Although racing's contribution to the advancement of technology is still far from insignificant there is no doubt that there is an increasing and inevitable divergence between racing cars and ordinary cars. Because of the desire for ever higher speeds racing car manufacturers choose solutions which would be difficult to adapt to ordinary cars. This is a situation that was brought about by the regulations which have been developed to govern racing competitions.

Whatever the case, there will always be the danger of men losing their lives as long as racing continues, but had it not been for these single-minded and fearless pioneers our own lives would not have been so changed since the beginning of the century. This is good so long as speed and the lust for power do not become the ultimate goal. These moral considerations aside, motor racing will continue to be a breath-taking spectacle, and the cars which take part, almost perfect examples of the technician's skill.

Ferruccio Bernabò

Left and above: Felice Nazzaro, winner of the 1907 Grand Prix at Dieppe. Nazzaro, who drove for Fiat for over fifteen years, was considered the finest driver of his generation. Centre: Vincenzo Lancia, nicknamed the 'Red Devil', who also drove for Fiat before himself becoming a car builder in 1907. Right: George Boillot, who was French champion in the years before the First World War, was the official driver for Peugeot.

The birth of motor racing

When the full powers of steam and electricity were finally realised it became apparent that here was a new method of transport which would carry man along at hitherto undreamed-of speeds. Self-powered road vehicles had been invented in the past, as early as 1769 when the Frenchman, Nicholas Cugnot from Lorraine, had built a heavy steam-powered tricycle. However it was not until 1885 and 1886 that the Germans, Carl Benz and Gottlieb Daimler, ran the first gasoline-engined carriages and, because of their perseverance in the face of enormous obstacles and cynicism, are now acclaimed as the leading contributors to the evolution of the motor car as we know it today.

The development of technical instruments and mechanical power excited the spirit of competition. The idea of travelling between two points, faster than anyone else had ever done, set men's imaginations alight and produced a breed of man utterly dedicated to the development and driving of these new machines. To begin with, the establishment of records was not covered by any precise regulations, but because of this competitive spirit it soon became necessary to compare speeds on the spot, and so the sport of motor racing began. The rules concerning mechanical aspects took much longer to acquire their ultimate importance.

The first races in the 1890s

Motor racing was born on 22 July 1894 with the organisation of the Paris-Rouen race run over 126 km (79 miles). It was won by a steam car built by De Dion and Bouton, driven by Count de Dion at 18.5 kmph (11.6 mph). But this was only a trial, and the first real motor race took place the following year in the Paris-Bordeaux-Paris run. This was won by a Panhard powered by a Daimler engine, which, in more than 48 hours of driving, made an average speed of 24 kmph (15 mph). The year 1895 also saw the first Italian run, Turin-Asti-Turin, which was won by a Daimler.

It was chiefly in France during the 90s and in the first years of this century that motor racing was developed with point-to-point races, usually starting from Paris. Panhard held the lead to begin with because of the successive increases in the size of their engines, but they failed to keep up with technical developments and faded from the racing scene within two or three years. Technical progress made on the actual machines resulted in regulations being laid down for all cars taking part. These were applied for the first time in the Gordon-Bennett Cup which came to be taken as the prototype of all motor races. The conditions for this cup, which was offered by the US newspaper proprietor James Gordon Bennett, were that any country could enter a team of three cars, every single part of which had to be made in that country. The races were run from 1900 for six years; but in 1906 the French automobile industry, which had grown remarkably, was no longer willing to be restricted to only three cars, and the first French Grand Prix open to all comers was run in that year.

1899: 100 kmph is attained

As early as 1898 Chasseloup-Laubat, in the electric Jeantaud, covered the distance of one kilometre in 57 seconds. This was the first officially registered 'time' in the world for a motor vehicle which gave a definite measure of the potential of this new means of travel. The next year Camille Jenatzy in the 'Jamais Contente', an electric car with storage batteries, managed to exceed 100 kmph and then, in 1902, reached 102 kmph in Leon Serpollet's steam car. In the following year piston engines such as the Mors and the Gobron-Brilliè reached 124 and 136 kmph respectively.

The eighth French Grand Prix in 1903, from Paris to Madrid, ended when the competitors had got only as far as Bordeaux because of a series of terrible accidents which claimed victims among both participants and public. This was the end of point-to-point racing, as European governments forbade any speed trials on public roads – which until then had seemed to be the obvious place. Nevertheless, the triumph of Gabriel who drove his Mors

 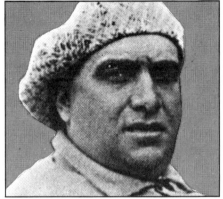 

Left: Leon Thery, winner of the 1905 Gordon Bennett Cup on the Auvergne circuit. Above: Pietro Bordino, who learnt racing driving from Vincenzo Lancia, and himself became an official driver for Fiat. Centre: Giuseppe Campari, one of the Alfa Romeo aces, who was killed during the Monza Grand Prix in 1933. Right: Antonio Ascari, killed at Monthlery during the Grand Prix of 1925. He was the father of Alberto Ascari, champion of the fifties.

at no less than 105 kmph (63.3 mph) for 545 km (342 miles) through this carnage will never be forgotten.

Special tracks were now built and the technical results of competitions began to assume importance over their sporting value. But technological advance was not confined to racing driving, and the construction of these record-breaking cars was the same as that of ordinary cars for the more leisurely public. When innovations were made it was natural that they should be tested in races, their success or failure depending on the results. Pneumatic tires were tested in this way, being used for the first time by Michelin in 1895. The combustion engine came to be decided upon in preference to steam or storage batteries because of the regulations for the first Grand Prix.

The changing nature of the sport

By the beginning of the First World War the automobile industry was producing cars at a capacity rate, and the publicity which was the inevitable follow-up of racing events proved to be of great value commercially. In return for supplying all the parts that are necessary for the building of a car, manufacturers received free advertising and sales-promotion, and had their products thoroughly tested on the tracks. All this helped to change the conception of racing driving as a pure sport and the personalities and skill of the drivers assumed secondary importance to the technological evolution of the machines with which they worked. Other sports in which amateurs took part did not have these commercial factors to reckon with, and motor racing began to seem very far removed from the idea of sport for its own sake.

Both the technical and sporting elements of racing had to conform to a careful set of regulations. National automobile clubs controlled racing events in their own countries, but all of them were co-ordinated through the Paris-based International Automobile Federation (Federation Internationale de l'Automobile: FIA) founded in 1904.

Other mechanical sports such as motor cycling and aviation developed more slowly. Although it started at the beginning of the century, motor cycling only really became established as a sport after 1910, with the setting up of national motor cycling clubs. Aviation, at first, seemed definable as a sport but was more concerned with the conquest of distance and altitude than with racing. Individual record-breaking attempts were made, but the more conventional type of race took place less often.

In France in 1923 the 24 hours at Le Mans was initiated. This race was a prolonged endurance test for the mechanics of sports cars, and it also helped to improve lighting techniques which up to then had been poor. The race is one in which technical development is of primary importance, and in which the results show how general production can be improved. In 1955 this event nearly came to an end when 83 people were killed and many more injured after one of the cars had smashed into the crowd. For months the future of this race was in the balance but it was resumed after the safety regulations had been strengthened. The Italian Mille Miglia had the same material advantages as the Le Mans but was stopped in 1957 after an accident in which the Marquis de Portago, his co-driver and many spectators were killed. The risks both to drivers and to the public had become excessive.

The evolution of the formulae

Because of the fundamental technical problems governing the designing and building of racing cars, international regulations have to lay down continually changing formulae and only those cars which comply with these limits are allowed to enter official races. It is this factor, above all else, which has made motor racing into a technical competition rather than a sport.

While motor racing was in its infancy every manufacturer was engaged in all kinds of experiment, and cars were built according to the designer's fancy. The first Grand Prix regulations, in 1898, merely divided the competitors into Heavy Cars (over 400 kg) and Voiturettes

Facing page: (above) Count Tchaikowski at the wheel of 8-cylinder Bugatti 4900, after setting a world record time of 216.610 on the Avus circuit near Berlin. (Below) Gigi Villoresi in the Maserati 1500, overall winner at the first postwar Grand Prix, Nice, 22 April 1946

Left: Rudolf Carraciola, German champion of the Mercedes team between 1926 and 1939. In 1932 he also drove for Alfa Romeo. Centre: Achille Varsi was one of the world's greatest racing drivers. He drove at various times for Alfa Romeo, Maserati, Bugatti and Auto-Union. Right: Tazio Nuvolari, the 'flying Mantuan', was, like Varsi, a great champion engaged for many of the *grandes marques*.

(100 to 400 kg); three years later the heavy category was further sub-divided into Heavy (over 650 kg) and Light (400 to 650 kg) cars. It was not until 1907 that any limitation on engine size was set, and this was expressed in terms of fuel consumption (20 litres per 100 km). The French had opened the Grand Prix competition to all comers in 1906, and by 1908 there was not a French car in the first three places, which were taken by Mercedes and two Benz cars; as a result, the race was not run again until 1912 when, with no Formula restrictions, Boillot's 7.6-litre Peugeot decisively defeated Wagner's 16-litre Fiat.

In 1913, the first practical limitations were imposed. Fuel consumption was restricted to 20 litres per 100 km (14.1 miles per gallon, 11.76 per US gallon); and the weight limits were between 800 and 1100 kg. Boillot repeated his 1912 success, and Jules Goux came second in another Peugeot.

From this time on, the formulae became gradually more and more precise in definition, imposing strict restrictions on weight, engine displacement, fuel consumption and car dimensions. Manufacturers were forced to work within these limits, but the formulae were constantly modified as new problems of limitation arose with each new technical advance.

These technical regulations were still based on the search for greater power and speed. The general tendency was to reduce weight and cubic capacity. The overall improvement of carburetors, lubricators, tires and lighter alloys, new discoveries in air cooling and heat transfer, and mechanical advances helped car builders to increase power in relation to the cubic capacity on more scientific lines. The best cars made between 1905 and 1910, with cubic capacities of more than 10 litres, gave 6 to 8 hp per litre at 1,400-1,600 rpm. A little before the First World War horsepower leapt up to 30 hp per litre at 3,000 rpm with engines of less than 5,000 cc produced by Peugeot and Mercedes. In 1920-21 the 3 litre cars made by Fiat and Duesenberg exceeded 4,000 rpm and reached 120 hp. Maximum speeds rose from 140 to 190 kmph and the dry weight fell from 1,800 to 1,100 kg.

Introduction of the supercharger

Engines were still to undergo great improvements in the unending search for perfection, but the basic mechanical structure was not to change. Superchargers were introduced in 1924-25 by Fiat, Alfa Romeo and Mercedes (but not adopted by Bugatti and Delage) as a method of increasing pressure (and therefore revolutions per minute) and horsepower, which in the 2-litre cars of that year rose to 5,500 rpm and 70-80 hp per litre respectively. Maximum speeds did not increase because of the cubic capacity limits imposed by the Grand Prix formula of those years, but there were noticeable general improvements in cars' stability, manageability and braking powers. Front-wheel brakes became general in 1920, although the 4.5-litre Peugeot had been fitted with them six years earlier. Tire resistance was no longer a problem, and in 1923 the design of the bodywork was improved when some French car manufacturers, in particular Bugatti and Voisin, brought out racing cars which showed the beginnings of streamlining.

From 1928-30 the Formula was not rigidly adhered to, and in the following three years no limitations were imposed at all. This resulted in a great increase in cubic capacity and the cars of these years had enormous but superfluous power. The FIA thought to curb these excesses by imposing a maximum dry weight of 750 kg without the tires. But the German firms, Mercedes and Auto-Union, had made such progress in metallurgical fields that they were capable of producing 5 or even 6-litre engines without exceeding the weight limit. Their tremendous 500 or 600 hp made these cars very difficult to drive and the old tracks were not up to their terrifying speeds. Moreover the chassis had become greatly modified due to the appearance of hydraulic brakes and independent suspension which demanded far less physical effort from the driver. All this technical advance meant that although sport was still a factor in motor racing, the main stimulant of competition

lay in technical rivalry, and the real battles were fought out. not on the circuits, but in the factories and on the drawing boards.

The resumption of racing after the Second World War

After the Second World War motor racing was resumed in 1946 with the Nice Grand Prix, which Luigi Villoresi won in a 1½-litre Maserati. Three weeks later the Marseilles Grand Prix was won by Raymond Sommer in a similar car. At first only a motley collection of pre-war cars competed: the 1938 1½-litre Alfa-Romeo team were brought out of storage and, on those occasions when they ran, dominated the races. Many of these first post-war events were virtually Free Formula, and most of the cars conformed to pre-war specifications, but a new formula was drawn up during 1947 and remained unchanged until the end of 1953. Of the pre-war *grandes marques* only Alfa-Romeo and (from 1954) Mercedes took part in Grand Prix races, but soon many small specialist firms began to devote themselves to the development of the racing car: Ferrari, in Italy, Cooper, BRM and Lotus in Britain, and the re-organised Porsche in Germany.

Under the new formula, the capacity of cars with superchargers was reduced to 1,500 cc, but the increase in specific power continued; for instance, the 1-litre Alfa-Romeo engine attained 380 hp. The supercharger was not widely used in commercial production, due to its high fuel consumption, and there was a move to dispense with it altogether, imposing a limit of 4½ litres, and 130 hp became a fair average.

Sports cars were developed on parallel lines with racing cars, mainly by MG, Aston-Martin, Jaguar, Triumph, etc. These included ordinary cars at the outset, but it was not long before prototypes were introduced, which began to bear a marked resemblance to Grand Prix cars. Sports cars were used mainly on roads over long distances or on short hill climbs, and more rarely on racing tracks.

Speed records

Record-breaking attempts are part of motor racing, but their significance is rather different, since they are concerned with the scientific measurement of the mechanical potentialities of the car engines. At first, of course, the attempt to reach ever greater speeds was a matter of simple human ambition; later the motive became one of technological, or even national, prestige, and cars were built expressly for the purpose of record attempts.

As early as 1909 Hémery established an absolute record for land-speed exceeding 200 kmph, and it was not until 1932 that this figure was doubled by Malcolm Campbell. Shortly before the Second World War John Cobb managed to reach 600 kmph and in 1947 he exceeded 634 kmph in a monstrous but carefully streamlined 2,600 hp car. From there Donald Campbell graduated to turbine engines, reaching 648 kmph, and finally Gary Gabelich passed the 1,000 kmph mark in the rocket-powered Blue Flame.

The formulae of recent years

Great technical progress has been made in racing cars since the mid-fifties, during which time three formulae have succeeded one another. From 1954 to 1960 a limit of 2,500 cc without supercharger was imposed, with an alternative of 7,500 cc with supercharger which was not taken up at all by the manufacturers. From 1961 to 1965 a maximum of 1,500 cc and a minimum weight of 450 kg was enforced, and finally, since 1966, regulations have laid down a maximum of 3,000 cc without supercharger, or 1,500 cc with supercharger, and a minimum weight of 500 kg. This weight has now been increased to allow for the additional safety equipment which has become mandatory.

In the first of these three periods an average of 260 hp was established, although from 1958 onwards the special methyl alcohol fuel permitted hitherto was banned in favour of 100/30 octane fuel, and disk brakes first appeared. These were a great step forward and also benefited some production line cars. In 1949 Alfa-Romeo had withdrawn

Facing page: Stirling Moss at the wheel of the single-seater Formula II HWM (2,000 cc), a British car in which he proved to be one of the greatest drivers of the 1950s

Left: Louis Chiron, from Monte Carlo, earned the nickname of 'wily old fox' for his tricky driving at the Nurburgring in 1934. A pre-war ace, he also had some success during 1946-49; but his greatest victories were for Bugatti. Centre: Bernd Rosemeyer of the Auto-Union team was killed on the Darmstadt-Frankfurt autobahn during a record-breaking attempt in 1938. Right: Hans von Stuck, who became Number One driver for Auto-Union in 1933.

from racing, possibly because they had lost their three great drivers: Achille Varsi, Wimille and Trossi; but then returned the following year, only to withdraw finally in 1952. However Mercedes-Benz made a comeback in 1954-55 with some exceptionally efficient cars. Lancia made an appearance alongside Ferrari, who were later to take over their cars after the death of Alberto Ascari. The British now began to make an impact on Grand Prix racing. Vanwall ran a full team of cars for only two years, but even this short time was sufficient to establish the excellence of British technique and to secure the Manufacturers' Championship in 1958 before the team retired again.

The new 1961 formula for 1,500 cc supercharged engines led to a decisive increase in specific power which exceeded 150 hp per litre thanks to engines reaching up to 1,200 rpm as in the case of the Honda. The extra power was the result of using multi-cylinder engines (mainly eight or twelve cylinders) with improved breathing and combustion, helped by the use of direct or indirect fuel injection, rather than of carburetors. This power could be exploited because of the progress made in streamlining, following the standardisation of the rear engine lay-out which had been introduced thirty years earlier by Auto-Union, but the value of which was established only in the fifties by the British manufacturer, Cooper. The increased lowering of the front part of racing cars led to the driver being placed in a totally artificial position: almost lying down.

The formula which was introduced in 1966 permitted the development of terrifying power. Already a car weighing little more than 500 kg had reached 420 hp. A new problem was raised: how to remain on the ground while travelling with such power. To give the driver more control cars were fitted with wheels with smaller diameters but with wider rims. In many cases the simple solution would have been to fit four-wheel drive; this however, would have led to enormous mechanical difficulties and a new style of driving, and so stabilising airfoils (which were to cause so much argument) were introduced. It is possible that, in this continuous search for power, the same dramatic situation that arose between 1934 and 1937 may occur again, when

the formula, which only limited the maximum weight to 750 kg, allowed for the development of huge engines; the situation could lead to a considerable increase in accidents, and it may become standard practice to introduce speed-limiting devices on circuits.

The prototypes

During the past few years regulation for sports cars have changed to much that the cars have deviated more and more from ordinary cars, from which, in fact, they should be derived. Thus a whole new category of 'prototypes' has come into being and the very name indicates the exceptional character of these machines: they are really two-seater racing cars. The freedom of choice regarding their cubic capacity has led to the production of extremely powerful cars, even faster at their top speed than the Formula I single seaters. The Ford which won the 24 Hours at Le Mans in 1968 was powered by a 7-litre 530 hp engine, and touched 340 kmph on the straight. This is the same as the take-off speed of a jet.

However, the International Trophy and races for these prototypes have introduced another World Championship and have led to the increasing popularity of racing driving.

The character of racing and the human factor

The technological importance of racing has decreased over the years, and the steady increase in speeds was hampered at one time by too many human and practical limitations. For a long time, however, the sport contributed greatly to the mechanical evolution of motor-powered vehicles by showing, far more quickly than any normal research could have done, how small and speedy engines, reliable brakes and high-resistance tires could be developed. There is, moreover, a certain interchange of ideas, and at times racing cars have acted as a sort of confirmatory trial for any innovations in the motor industry.

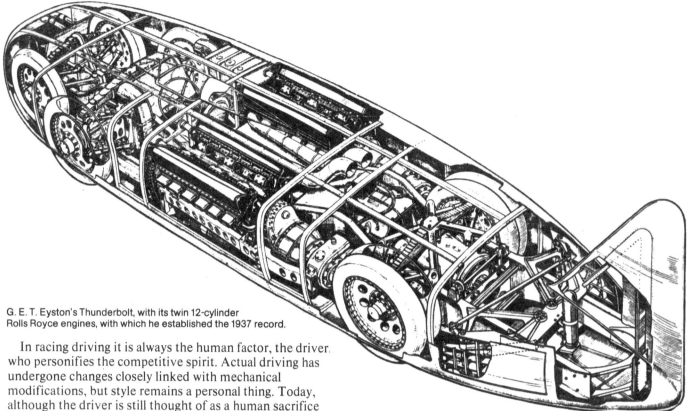

G. E. T. Eyston's Thunderbolt, with its twin 12-cylinder
Rolls Royce engines, with which he established the 1937 record.

In racing driving it is always the human factor, the driver.
who personifies the competitive spirit. Actual driving has
undergone changes closely linked with mechanical
modifications, but style remains a personal thing. Today,
although the driver is still thought of as a human sacrifice
to mechanical progress, the feeling of being a pioneer has
been dead a long time.

A large section of the public follows racing events as an
entertainment and an emotional outlet, but despite the
dangers the spectacular aspect has diminished, and the
technical side is limited now to the testing of accessories.
The enormous power of modern racing cars is out of touch
with reality. The danger of such high speeds has resulted in
roads being almost entirely abandoned in favour of race
tracks and formulae have been introduced, just as at the
start of motor racing, which limit speed and give it
technical validity. It is therefore hard to be objective in
defining the importance of this mechanical sport a century
after the invention of the combustion engine, and more
than seventy years after the appearance of the first
automobile. Averages of 220 kmph mean little to the new
generation when aeroplanes reach speeds of over
1,000 kmph and the new propulsion engines move space
missiles at many times the speed of sound.

The conquest of other worlds is also one of the motives
of motor racing. This combines both scientific and human
endeavour, and the sporting instincts of our predecessors
still play a certain part. The space ship is only a machine
with a driver, and, as such, a comparable prodigy to the
horseless carriage as it first appeared eighty years ago.

Metric equivalents

1 litre = 0.220 British gallon
= 0.264 US gallon
10 litres per 100 km = 28.2 mpg (British) = 23.5 mpg (US)
1 kilogram = 2.20 lb
1 metre = 3 ft 3.4 ins
1 cm = 0.394 inches
1 kilometre = 0.62 mile

World champion drivers

Year	Driver	Car	Year	Driver	Car
1950	Guiseppe Farina	Alfa Romeo	1962	Graham Hill	BRM
1951	Manuel Fangio	Ferrari	1963	Jim Clark	Lotus
1952	Alberto Ascari	Ferrari	1964	John Surtees	Ferrari
1953	Alberto Ascari	Ferrari	1965	Jim Clark	Lotus
1954	Juan Manuel Fangio	Maserati and Mercedes	1966	Jack Brabham	Brabham
1955	Juan Manuel Fangio	Mercedes	1967	Denny Hulme	Brabham
1956	Juan Manuel Fangio	Ferrari	1968	Graham Hill	Lotus
1957	Juan Manuel Fangio	Maserati	1969	Jackie Stewart	Matra-Ford
1958	Mike Hawthorn	Ferrari	1970	Jochen Rindt	Lotus-Ford
1959	Jack Brabham	Cooper	1971	Jackie Stewart	Tyrrell-Ford
1960	Jack Brabham	Cooper	1972	Emerson Fittipaldi	JPS-Lotus
1961	Phil Hill	Ferrari			

The land speed record

Year	Driver / Vehicle (Location)	mph	kmph
1898	Chasseloup-Laubat in the Jeantaud (Achères, France)	39.2	63.157
1899	Jenatzy in the Jenatzy (Achères, France)	41.4	66.645
1899	Chasseloup-Laubat in the Jeantaud (Achères, France)	43.5	70.297
1899	Jenatzy in the Jenatzy (Achères, France)	49.8	80.321
1899	Chasseloup-Laubat in the Jeantaud (Achères, France)	58.1	93.724
1899	Jenatzy in the Jenatzy (Achères, France)	65.8	105.904
1902	Serpollet in the Serpollet (Nice, France)	75.1	120.771
1902	Fournier in the Mors (Dourdan, France)	76.6	123.249
1902	Augères in the Mors (Dourdan, France)	77.1	124.102
1903	Duray in the Gobron-Brillié (Ostend, Belgium)	84.6	136.330
1903	Henry Ford in a Ford 999 (Lake Saint Clair, USA)	91.4	147.014
1904	W. K. Vanderbilt in a Mercedes (Daytona Beach, USA)	92.2	148.510
1904	Rigoly in the Gobron-Brillié (Nice, France)	94.8	152.501
1904	De Caters in a Mercedes (Ostend, Belgium)	97.5	156.911
1904	Rigoly in the Gobron-Brillié (Ostend, Belgium)	103.5	166.628
1904	Baras in a Darracq (Mongeron, France)	104.5	168.188
1905	Arthur MacDonald in a Napier (Daytona Beach, USA)	104.7	168.381
1905	Hémery in a Darracq (Aries-Salon, France)	109.0	175.422
1909	Hémery in a Benz (Brooklands, England)	125.9	202.655
1910	Barney Oldfield in a Benz (Daytona Beach, USA)	131.1	211.500
1922	K. L. Guinness in a Sunbeam (Brooklands, England)	133.8	215.250
1924	René Thomas in a Delage (Arpajon, France)	143.1	230.634
1924	E. A. D. Aldridge in a Fiat (Arpajon, France)	146.0	234.986
1924	Campbell in a Sunbeam (Pendine Sands, Wales)	146.1	235.217
1925	Campbell in a Sunbeam (Pendine Sands, Wales)	150.9	242.800
1926	Segrave in a Sunbeam (Southport, England)	152.1	245.149
1926	J. G. Parry-Thomas in a Thomas Special (Pendine Sands, Wales)	171.1	275.229
1927	M. Campbell in a Napier Campbell (Pendine Sands, Wales)	174.9	281.447
1927	H. O. D. Segrave in a Sunbeam (Daytona Beach, USA)	203.8	327.981
1928	M. Campbell in a Napier-Campbell (Daytona Beach, USA)	206.9	333.062
1928	Ray Keechosu, White-Triples (Daytona Beach, USA)	207.7	334.022
1929	H. O. D. Segrave in an Irving-Napier (Daytona Beach, USA)	231.4	372.340
1931	Sir Malcolm Campbell in a Napier-Campbell (Daytona Beach, USA)	246.1	395.469
1932	Sir Malcolm Campbell in a Napier-Campbell (Bonneville Salt Flats, USA)	254.0	408.621
1933	Sir Malcolm Campbell in a Rolls-Royce Campbell (Daytona Beach, USA)	272.5	438.123
1935	Sir Malcolm Campbell in the Bluebird Special (Bonneville Salt Flats, USA)	301.3	484.818
1937	G.E.T. Eyston in Thunderbolt (Bonneville Salt Flats, USA)	311.9	501.374
1938	John Cobb in a Railton (Bonneville Salt Flats, USA)	350.2	563.577
1938	G. E. T. Eyston in Thunderbolt (Bonneville Salt Flats, USA)	357.5	575.217
1939	John Cobb in a Railton (Bonneville Salt Flats, USA)	369.7	593.560
1947	John Cobb in a Railton (Bonneville Salt Flats, USA)	394.2	634.267
1964	Donald Campbell in Bluebird II (Lake Eyre, Australia)	403.1	648.728
1964	Bob Summers in Goldenrod (Bonneville Salt Flats, USA)	409.3	658.621
1964	Craig Breedlove in Spirit of America (Bonneville Salt Flats, USA)	526.3	843.590
1964	Art Arfons in Green Monster (Bonneville Salt Flats, USA)	536.7	863.570
1965	Craig Breedlove in Spirit of America (Bonneville Salt Flats, USA)	555.0	893.390
1965	Art Arfons in Green Monster (Bonneville Salt Flats, USA)	576.3	927.846
1965	Craig Breedlove in Spirit of America (Bonneville Salt Flats, USA)	600.6	966.602
1970	G. Gabelich in Blue Flame (Bonneville Salt Flats, USA)	622.4	1001.628

The development of Formula 1

1906	Maximum weight: 1,000 kg, plus 7 kg for the magneto ignition. The horn, safety equipment, headlights and their supports, interior fittings and tool box (unless this was used as a seat) are not included in the weight of the chassis. The exhaust pipes must be horizontal with the ends curving backwards and up to avoid collecting dust from the roads. Two drivers, each weighing no more than 60 kg.
1907	Fuel consumption limited to 9.4 mpg (7.84 per US gallon; 30 litres to the 100 km). No restrictions placed on weight or cubic capacity.
1908	Minimum weight: 1,100 kg. No restrictions on rpm, but 4 cylinder engines limited to 155 mm bore. Other numbers of cylinders have proportional limits. The weight does not include water, fuel, tools, safety equipment or the spare wheel.
1909–1911	No formula during this time.
1912	Free formula.
1913	Minimum weight: 800 kg: maximum weight: 1,100 kg. Fuel consumption restricted to 14.1 mpg (11.76 per US gallon; 20 litres to the 100 km).
1914	Minimum weight: 1,100 kg. Cubic capacity limited to 4,500 cc.
1915–1919	No formula.
1920	No formula. In the United States the cubic capacity is limited to 3,000 cc.
1921	No formula. In the United States the cubic capacity is limited to 3,000 cc. Minimum weight: 800 kg.
1922–1924	Cubic capacity: 2,000 cc. Minimum weight: 650 kg. The back of the car must not extend more than 150 cm (60 inches) beyond the centre of the rear axle. Two passengers (the driver and a mechanic) with a total weight not exceeding 120 kg.
1925	Cubic capacity: 2,000 cc. Minimum weight: 650 kg. The two-seater body to be no narrower than 80 cm (32 inches). Only one person to be aboard (this rule still applies).
1926	Cubic capacity: 1,500 cc. Minimum weight: 600 kg. Two-seater body to have minimum width of 80 cm (32 inches).
1927	Cubic capacity: 1,500 cc. Minimum weight: 700 kg. Two-seater or single-seater body to have minimum width of 85 cm (34 inches).
1928	No restrictions on the cylinders. Minimum weight: 550 kg. Maximum weight: 750 kg. Minimum length of track: 600 km.
1929	No restrictions on the cylinders. Minimum weight: 900 kg. Fuel consumption fixed at 14 kg (30.9 lbs) for combined gas and oil per 100 km. Minimum width 100 cm (40 inches).
1930	Lowest cubic capacity: 1,100 cc. Same fuel consumption as in 1929, but with an allowance of up to 30% of benzole.
1931	Free formula. Minimum duration of race: 10 hours. A co-driver obligatory.
1932	Free formula. Minimum duration of race: 5 hours; maximum: 10 hours.
1933	Free formula. Minimum length of race: 500 km.
1934–1937	No restrictions placed on cubic capacity. Maximum dry weight: 750 kg. Minimum width of body: 85 cm (34 inches). No restrictions placed on fuel.
1938–1940	Minimum cubic capacity: 769 cc with supercharger; maximum: 3,000 cc. Minimum cubic capacity: 1,000 cc without supercharger; maximum: 4,500 cc. Minimum weight excluding wheels: 400–850 kg according to the cubic capacity. No restrictions placed on fuel.
1947–1953	Cubic capacity restricted to: 1,500 cc with supercharger; 4,500 cc without supercharger. No restrictions on weight or fuel.
1954–1960	Cubic capacity restricted to: 2,500 cc without supercharger; 750 cc with supercharger. No restrictions on weight or fuel: after 1958, only 100/130 octane aviation spirit.
1961–1965	Maximum cubic capacity: 1,500 cc; minimum: 1,300; without supercharger. Minimum weight 450 kg (992 lbs) with oil and water but without gas. Ballast forbidden for increasing weight; commercial fuel; automatic starter; double brakes; refuelling during the race forbidden; safety belts; safety fuel tank; open cockpit; exposed wheels. These were the main regulations laid down by the International Automobile Federation to increase the safety of cars and racing.
1966–1973	Maximum cubic capacity: 1,500 cc with supercharger; 3,000 cc without supercharger. Commercial fuel; minimum weight with oil and water, but no fuel: 500 kg. Weight increased by 30 kg for mandatory safety equipment and this allowance subsequently increased to 50 kg.

Some important GP cars:1907-1939

Make and type	Year	Cylinders	Cubic capacity	HP	RPM	HP per litre	Weight
Fiat 130 HP	1907	4	16,286	130	1,600	8	1,025
Peugeot	1912	4	7,600	130	2,200	17	1.480
Delage	1913	4	6,200	105	2,300	16	1.460
Mercedes GP	1914	4	4,483	115	2,800	26	1.070
Fiat 805	1923	8	1,979	130	5,500	66	680
Alfa Romeo P 2	1924	8	1,987	140	5,500	70	750
Fiat 806	1927	12	1,484	180	7,500	118	700
Bugatti 35 C	1930	8	1,955	130	5,300	65	765
Alfa Romeo P 3	1932	8	2,654	210	5,600	81	700
Auto-Union C	1936	16 V	6,006	520	5,000	86	748
Mercedes W 125	1937	8	5,660	640	5,800	114	750
Maserati 8 CTF	1938	8	2,991	420	6,800	140	750
Mercedes	1939	8 V	1,492	270	6,500	180	690

1946-1960

Make and type	Year	Cylinders	Cubic capacity	HP	RPM	HP per litre	Weight kg
Maserati 4 CLT	1946	4	1,484	270	7,000	180	680
Alfa Romeo 159	1951	8	1,479	420	9,300	287	710
Ferrari 375	1951	12 V	4,494	380	7,500	85	720
Mercedes	1954	8	2,496	275	9,000	110	635
Lancia	1954	8 V	2,487	265	8,500	106	620
Vanwall	1957	4	2,488	285	7,100	114	630
Maserati 250 F	1957	6	2,493	270	7,500	108	640
Cooper-Climax	1960	4	2,495	240	6,800	96	500

Since 1960

Make and type	Year	Cylinders	Cubic capacity	HP	RPM	HP per litre	Weight kg
Ferrari 156	1961	6 V	1,477	190	9,500	128	460
Lotus 25	1963	8 V	1,498	185	9,000	123	450
BRM	1964	8 V	1,497	200	10,000	133	470
Ferrari 512	1965	12 F	1,490	220	12,000	147	465
Honda	1967	12 V	2,994	400	11,000	133	650
Brabham-Repco	1967	8 V	2,994	345	9,000	114	540
Ferrari	1967	12 V	2,989	390	10,000	130	550
Honda	1968	8 V	2,833	365	10,000	121	500
Lotus-Ford	1967–1968	8 V	2,993	415	9,500	142	520
Matra	1969	12 V	3,000	300–350	12,000	100–110	500
Lotus-Ford	1970	8 V	2,993	430	10,000	143	530
Ferrari	1971	12 F	2,998	475	12,000	158	540
Tyrell-Ford	1971	8 V	2,993	440	10,000	147	540
BRM	1971	12 V	2,998	445	10,500	148	530

1 The Itala of the famous 1907 Peking-Paris run. This trial, organized by the newspaper *Le Matin*, matched the Italian car of Prince Scipione Borghese (who was accompanied by the mechanic Ettore Guizzardi and Luigi Barzini, special envoy of the *Corriere della Sera*) against two de Dion-Boutons, a Conte tricycle and a Spyker. The start took place in Peking on 10 June, 1907. The Itala rapidly out-distanced all its opponents and after many adventures (described by Barzini in his book, 'Half the World Seen From a Motor Car') it reached Paris. The journey was nearly 10,000 miles and took exactly two months. The Itala was a 35/45 hp model with a 4-cylinder engine of 7,433 cc; weight 1,370 kg and a maximum speed of 100 kmph. (Automobile Museum, Turin.)

2 The 130 hp Fiat driven by Felice Nazzaro which, in 1907, won the Grand Prix de l'Automobile Club de France on the Dieppe circuit. This car is now in the Automobile Museum in Turin. It has a 4-cylinder engine; bore and stroke 180x160 mm; capacity 16,186 cc; 130 hp at 1,600 rpm; chain drive and a maximum speed of 160 kmph. (Automobile Museum, Turin.)

3

4

5

3 Vincenzo Lancia, with mechanic Pietro Bordino, at the wheel of the Fiat 100 hp. This car was built in 1905 with 4 cylinders; capacity 16,286 cc.

4 The impressive Fiat S 76 made in 1911. It had a 4-cylinder engine of 28,353 cc; 290 hp and a maximum speed of 210 kmph.

5 The 1914 Mercedes in which Lautenschläger won the Grand Prix de l'Automobile Club de France on 4 July, 1914, a few days before war was declared. Lautenschläger made an average speed of 105.550 kmph.

6   Pietro Bordino in a Fiat taking a corner of the Strasburg circuit in the Grand Prix de l'Automobile Club de France in 1922. The race was won by Nazzaro, also in a Fiat, although Bordino drove the lap record of 138.810 kmph. The competition Fiat in 1922 was the 804 model with a 6-cylinder engine of 1,991 cc and 110 hp at 5,000 rpm.

7   The Alfa Romeo P1 in the European Grand Prix at Monza in 1923. Antonio Ascari, who is at the wheel, was killed in a crash at Monthléry in 1925. Designed by Vittorio Jano, this car had a 6-cylinder 2-litre engine with supercharger, and developed 116 hp at 5,000 rpm.

8   The Itala 11, a revolutionary car made in 1925 and designed by Giulio Cesare Cappa. It had a 12-cylinder V-shaped engine of 1,100 cc developing 60 hp, front wheel drive, independent suspension on all four wheels and a wooden chassis, but was never used for racing purposes. (Automobile Museum, Turin.)

7

8

9

10

11

9 The 1923 Fiat 805 with Pietro Bordino at the wheel. This model was the first racing car to have a supercharger. The straight 8-cylinder engine of 1,979 cc developed 150 hp at 5,500 rpm. Carlo Salamano won the 1923 European Grand Prix at Monza in this car.

10 The Alfa Romeo P2 which, between 1924–1930, won nearly all the big races. It had an 8-cylinder engine with a supercharger, capacity of 1,987 cc, 140 hp. The 1930 model, shown here, developed 175 hp. (Automobile Museum, Turin.)

11 An 8-cylindered Maserati 2500 in front of the pits during trials before the 1930 Monza Grand Prix. On the right Achille Varzi is looking at the car in which he was to win the race a few days later.

12 The strange Trossi-Monaco racing car, made in 1935 by Count Carlo Felice Trossi, one of the best drivers of his time, and the engineer Augusto Monaco. It had a radial 16-cylinder two-stroke, air-cooled engine, capacity 3,982 cc, and developed 250 hp at 6,000 rpm. As it never reached a sufficient standard, this car was not raced in competitions, although it took part in the trials for the 1935 Italian Grand Prix. (Automobile Museum, Turin.)

13 Achille Varsi, with the mechanic Bignami, at the wheel of the 6-cylinder Maserati Sport (3,724 cc), goes through the Futa Pass in the 1935 Mille Miglia. Shortly after this picture was taken he retired from the race, which was won by Pintacuda-Della Stufa in an Alfa Romeo 2900, with an average speed of 114.750 kmph.

14 The 'bi-motor' Alfa Romeo driven by Tazio Nuvolari, which reached 338 kmph in 1935 on the Bergamo-Brescia autoroute. This car had two 8-cylinder engines, one in the traditional position and the other mounted at the rear, giving a capacity of 6,330 cc, and 530 hp; dry weight was 1,030 kg.

13   14

15

15 The 1937 racing Mercedes. With a straight 8-cylinder engine, capacity 5,600 cc with supercharger, it developed a maximum 630 hp at 5,800 rpm. At this time the superiority of German cars in Grand Prix was obvious. Enormous sums had been put at the disposal of Mercedes and Auto-Union as propaganda for the Third Reich. Alfa Romeo and Maserati tried to compete, but with little success.

16 The Mercedes-Benz GP of the 1938–1940 formula, 3 litres supercharged or 4 litres without supercharger. It was powered by a 12-cylinder, V-shaped engine with a two-stage supercharger, and developed up to 460 hp at 7,800 rpm.

17 Bernd Rosemeyer in an Auto-Union during practice before the 1936 Pescara Grand Prix. Thanks to the 1934–1937 formula, which allowed a maximum dry weight of 750 kg, huge engines were built at this time. A V-shaped engine of 16 cylinders, capacity 6 litres and developing 510 hp, was fitted at the rear of the 1936 Auto-Union. Rosemeyer was a great champion despite his brief career. He died in 1938 during an unlucky record-breaking attempt on the Darmstadt-Frankfurt autobahn.

17

18 The Auto-Union built for the 3-litre formula of 1937–1940. It had a 12-cylinder engine in the rear, and was provided with a supercharger; it developed nearly 420 hp.

19 Herman Müller, winner of the French Grand Prix at Reims in 1939, in an Auto-Union 3000. Auto-Union was a partnership of the Audi, DKW, Horch and Wanderer firms. The first racing car of this German marque was designed by Professor Ferdinand Porsche, one of the greatest authorities on automobile mechanics, who later devoted himself entirely to the development of the 'people's car': the Volkswagen. The development of Auto-Union racing cars was then handed over to the engineer, Eberan von Eberhorst.

20 The 1939 racing Maserati which had an 8-cylinder engine, 3,000 cc with supercharger. This car, driven by Wilbur Shaw, won the famous Indianapolis 500 two years running, in 1939 and 1940.

21 The 1936 Austin OHC, a small British racing car. It had a 4-cylinder engine of 750 cc exceeding 10,000 rpm. This car was only used in English races, of which it won several.

22 23

22 The 1938–1940 formula Alfa Romeo 316 which had a 6-cylinder engine of 3,000 cc. With its 430 hp it was a credit to the Italians who were faced with competition from the powerful German cars.

23 Nino Farina in the 1948 Maserati. This car was a 4 CLT model with a 4-cylinder engine and supercharger, developing up to 270 hp.

24 Alberto Ascari in the Ferrari 2000. This Italian driver won the world championship twice in this car, in 1952 and 1953.

25 The 1946 model of the famous Alfa Romeo 158 (also known as the Alfetta) derived from a 1938 model of the same name. It had a straight 8-cylinder engine of 1,500 cc with a supercharger. Its original 190 hp developed progressively to 270 hp and 350 hp, and finally reached 420 hp. With drivers such as Varzi, Farina, Trossi and Wimille, the Alfa 158 (later 159) led the field between 1946 and 1951. (Automobile Museum, Turin.)

24

25

26 Formula II cars (2,000 cc without supercharger) fought each other in the 1952 and 1953 Grand Prix. The illustration shows the Formula II Ferrari which won nearly all the big races during these two years; bore and stroke 90x78 mm, 1,985 cc, developing 180 hp. (Automobile Museum, Turin.)

27 The Cisitalia GP, built between 1948 and 1949, had to be abandoned while still being developed, owing to disputes in the firm making it, which had been founded by Piero Dusio. The design of the GP was entrusted to Porsche's top team of technicians. The car had a 12-cylinder, horizontally-opposed rear engine of 1,500 cc with a double supercharger, giving over 300 hp at 8,500 rpm. A notable feature was the four-wheel transmission, which could be applied, if necessary, to the back axle only.

27

28

29

28 The Lancia Sport Carrera model in which Fangio won the famous 1954 Carrera Panamericana in Mexico over a total of 3,077 km; he averaged 169.230 kmph. The car had a V6 engine with 60 degrees of inclination, 3,100 cc developing 235 hp. The following year Alberto Ascari won the twenty-first Mille Miglia in a Lancia modelled on the Carrera. (Automobile Museum, Turin.)

29 In 1954 Mercedes-Benz returned to Grand Prix racing with two different versions of a car with an 8-cylinder, 2,500 cc engine: one with streamlined bodywork, and the other with exposed wheels. The illustration shows a group of streamlined Mercedes in the Berlin Grand Prix on the Avus circuit. Karl Kling, who won the race with an average speed of 213.500 kmph, is in the lead.

30 The Formula I Mercedes 2500 with exposed wheels. Driving in one or the other version, the Argentinian Juan-Manuel Fangio won the world championship in 1954 and 1955.

30

31

31 The D-type Jaguar sports car in which Hawthorn and Bueb won the 1955 Twenty-four Hour Le Mans. This British car, and its predecessor the C-type, also won the 1951, 1953, 1956 and 1957 Le Mans, powered by a 6-cylinder engine initially 3.4 litres and later enlarged to 3.8 litres. The Jaguar C-type was the first car to be fitted with disc brakes. Until then they had been used only in the aircraft industry. (Automobile Museum, Turin.)

32 Alberto Ascari in a Ferrari battling with Fangio's Mercedes in the 1954 Italian Grand Prix, which was won by the great Argentinian.

33 The 1954–1960 Formula I Maserati with a 2,500 cc, 6-cylinder, 290 hp engine. In 1957 Fangio won his fifth world championship in this car. (Automobile Museum, Turin.)

32

33

34   The 1955 Formula I Lancia with its two side-mounted petrol
tanks. Designed by Vittorio Jano this Italian car is powered by
a V8 engine with a cubic capacity of 2,500 cc developing 264 hp
at 8,500 rpm. Alberto Ascari won the 1955 Naples and Turin Grand
Prix races with this Lancia. After his tragic death Lancia presented
the car to Ferrari. (Automobile Museum, Turin.)

35   The 1957 Formula II Ferrari (1,500 cc) at the Modena Grand
Prix, run on the 'Aerautodromo' of the racing car capital. It was
won by Jean Behra in a Maserati.

36–39   The 500 Miles was run on the Monza track, with its
famous 'wall' curve, in 1957 and 1958. American cars and drivers
from Indianapolis took part. Top picture shows the winner,
Troy Ruttman, with an average speed of 257.590 kmph. Among
the other cars is Jimmy Bryan's number 1, the Dean Van Lines
Special which won the Indianapolis 500 the following year.

36

37

38

39

40

40 The 1957 Formula I Ferrari which had a V8 engine of 2,492 cc, bore and stroke 80x62 mm, developing 280 hp at 9,000 rpm. That year Ferrari's team drivers included Luigi Musso, Peter Collins, Mike Hawthorn and Wolfgang von Trips. Although it did well in the world championship Grand Prix races, the single seater Ferrari could not compete with the Fangio-Maserati combination. The 1957 Formula I cars were all of traditional build: engine in front with transmission to the rear wheels. The rear engine was only re-introduced two years later by the British firm, Cooper.

41 Fangio in a Maserati at the gasworks corner during the 1957 Monaco Grand Prix. On the circuit running round the town of Monte Carlo the Argentinian champion, who that year won his fifth World Championship, managed to avoid a collision between Moss, Collins and Hawthorn, thus taking the lead which he kept to the end.

42 The straight 6-cylinder engine of the Maserati Formula I 2500 which won nearly all the great races in 1957.

4

42

43 The 1957 Modena Grand Prix, the last race of the season.
Pictured here are three cars coming out of the S bend:
Bonnier's BRM, Behra's Maserati and Musso's Ferrari.

44 Stirling Moss in a Vanwall, winner of the 1957 Italian
Grand Prix with an average speed of 193.563 kmph. The
British car had a 4-cylinder engine of 2,489 cc, bore and
stroke 96x86 mm, developing 290 hp at 8,000 rpm.

45 The 1959 Cooper during the trials for the Monaco
Grand Prix with Stirling Moss at the wheel. He led the race
until his transmission broke down in the 82nd lap. Jack
Brabham was the winner in another Cooper.

46

47

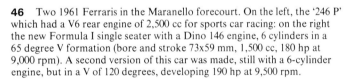

46 Two 1961 Ferraris in the Maranello forecourt. On the left, the '246 P' which had a V6 rear engine of 2,500 cc for sports car racing: on the right the new Formula I single seater with a Dino 146 engine, 6 cylinders in a 65 degree V formation (bore and stroke 73x59 mm, 1,500 cc, 180 hp at 9,000 rpm). A second version of this car was made, still with a 6-cylinder engine, but in a V of 120 degrees, developing 190 hp at 9,500 rpm.

47 Jack Brabham's Lotus-Climax (1962): the Australian left Cooper to drive a privately entered Lotus. He became a car builder and won the World Championship in a Brabham in 1966, having held the title twice before for Cooper, in 1959 and 1960.

48 The 1961 Monaco Grand Prix showing Dan Gurney's Porsche leading from John Surtees's Lola. The German Formula I car had a horizontally-opposed 4-cylinder rear engine.

49 Cars entering the Curva Parabolica at Monza during the 1958 Italian Grand Prix. From left to right: a Ferrari, a Vanwall and a Maserati fight it out side by side. Tony Brooks won the race in a Vanwall with an average speed of over 195 kmph.

49

50

50 The 1963 Monaco Grand Prix with John
Surtees in a Ferrari on the Tobacco corner.
It was the former motorcycle world champion's
first season in the Ferrari team but he was
never lucky on the Monaco circuit. That year
Surtees was fourth with the fastest lap time of
119.800 kmph. The race was won by Graham
Hill in a BRM with an average speed of
116.910 kmph. The 1961 Formula I Ferrari had
a 20 degree V 6-cylinder engine (1,476 cc, bore
and stroke 73x58.8 mm, direct fuel injection,
210 hp at 10,200 rpm), and weighed 480 kg.

51 Richie Ginther in a BRM taking the
Casino bend during the trials for the 1962
Monaco Grand Prix. He had an accident in the
first lap of the race but suffered no serious
consequences. The Formula I BRM of that year
had a V8 engine of 1,498 cc, with indirect fuel
injection, and developed 195 hp at 9,500 rpm.
It won the Italian Grand Prix at Monza with
Graham Hill and Richie Ginther taking the first
two places.

51

52 Jack Brabham in the Formula I single-seater which he designed and made himself in 1963. It had a V8 Coventry Climax engine of 1,496 cc, bore and stroke 67.8x51.6 mm, with direct fuel injection, and developed 240 hp at 9,800 rpm, the car weighing 485 kg.

53 Ferrari started the 1963 season with a 6-cylinder car which, driven by Surtees, was often well placed and had a resounding victory at the Nürburgring German Grand Prix. The Modena factory had made a new V8 engine for the Italian Grand Prix but it was not ready in time. (Automobile Museum, Turin.)

54 The 1964 Monaco Grand Prix, showing the cars stringing out soon after the start of the race. On the short, straight stretch following the terrible downhill chicane, Peter Arundell in a Lotus leads from the no. 20 Ferrari driven by Lorenzo Bandini. The race was won, after a series of incidents, by Graham Hill in a BRM.

55

55 The 1964 Formula I Cooper. John Cooper retained the tubular chassis on this car, but reinforced it with a very thin outer steel plate. The engine was the usual 90 degree V 8-cylinder, Coventry Climax type.

56 Richie Ginther at the wheel of a Honda during the 1965 Italian Grand Prix. The Japanese firm, Honda, having won successive victories in motor cycle racing, launched itself into the more difficult world of the Formula I. It had a hesitant start, but it was not long before the Japanese single-seaters were numbered amongst the fastest racing cars. The 1965 Mexican Grand Prix was won by a Honda.

57 In 1964 the BRM (seen here at Monza during practice for the Italian Grand Prix) was fitted with a new chassis on the same lines as that of the Lotus monocoque structure. This technique was then adopted by all makes of racing car.

58 Graham Hill and Jackie Stewart, both in BRMs, going round the Tobacco corner on the Monaco track in 1965. This was the last year of the 1500 formula.

57

58

59 The Scottish champion Jackie Stewart made his name during the 1965 season. He is seen here driving a BRM in the Monaco Grand Prix of that year.

60 The Dino 206 Ferrari in which Ludovico Scarfiotti won the European Mountain Championship in 1965 and 1966, beating the Porsche team. This car originally had a 65 degree V 6-cylinder rear engine of 1,593 cc which was then raised to 1,987 cc, giving 218 hp at 9,000 rpm. It weighed 580 kg.

61 A wheel to wheel battle between Jackie Stewart in a BRM (no. 32) and Jim Clark in a Lotus (no. 24) at the beginning of the Curva Parabolica on the Monza track in the 1965 Italian Grand Prix. Stewart was the victor.

62 The eve of every race is always a hectic time in the pits at Monza. Technicians and mechanics work night and day, minutely checking the smallest details and often making important last-minute modifications prompted by the results of the official trials. An expert checks the tyre pressure on Clark's Lotus.

62

63 The 1964 Italian Grand Prix at Monza with the winner, John Surtees, in a Ferrari. This car had a 12-cylinder engine, bore and stroke 56x50.4 mm, 1,489 cc, compression ratio 9.8:1, 220 hp at 1,200 rpm, and direct fuel injection (Lucas's system). The car weighed 465 kg and had a maximum speed of 260 kmph. Surtees won the race with an average speed of 205.63 kmph, and went on to win that year's World Championship.

64 Lorenzo Bandini in the 1966 12-cylinder Ferrari of 3,000 cc. The 3 litre formula came into its own that year, and the Italian Grand Prix was won by Ludovico Scarfiotti in this type of car.

65

66

65–66 Two versions of the 1967 BRM Formula I; above: the old model driven by Jackie Stewart in the Monaco Grand Prix. It was powered by a V8 engine of the previous formula (1,500 cc) but increased in capacity to 2 litres; below: the model powered by the H 16 engine; its 16 cylinders were arranged in two superimposed rows of 8 horizontal cylinders: a very interesting system from a technical viewpoint, but one that did not give the hoped-for results to the English firm.

67 A Lotus-BRM. Lotus, after having adopted the BRM engine in 1966, subsequently took up the Ford but still with the same 90 degree inclination of the cylinders. In the latter car in 1967 the great Jim Clark won the Netherlands, British, United States and Mexican Grands Prix, but failed, however, to beat the New Zealander, Denis Hulme, who, although he won only two races, scored sufficient high placings in other GP races to secure the world championship.

68–69 From 1966 the Cooper was fitted with a V12 Maserati engine which was later improved by the addition of a new 3-valved cylinder head, and by making the engine 'squarer', with bore and stroke 75.2x56 mm (in place of 70.4x64 mm); this increased hp to 380 at 9,000 rpm.

70 Chris Amon's Ferrari V12 on the straight stretch in front of the stands during the dramatic 1967 Monaco Grand Prix. Lorenzo Bandini, the best Italian driver of the last decade, was killed during the race. An instant before the accident he was in second place behind Hulme. Amon was third, two laps behind the winner.

71–72 Exhaust pipes and engine of the 12-cylinder Ferrari.

68

71 72

73

73–74 The 1967 Brabham Repco in which Denis Hulme and the maker, Jack Brabham, took first and second places in the World Championship. The engine, which was made in Australia by Repco from a stock American V8, had a single overhead camshaft for each bank of cylinders, bore and stroke 88x60.3 mm, 2,994 cc, maximum horsepower 340 hp at 9,000 rpm. In spite of their lack of power, the Brabhams won, thanks to their lightness and mechanical performance.

74

75

76

75–76 The Formula I Eagle, built by Anglo-American Racers, which won a single victory at Spa-Francorchamps in 1967, driven by Dan Gurney. The engine, made by Weslake, was a V12 and developed over 400 hp. On the whole this beautiful American single-seater turned out to be too fragile. It was driven in the Italian Grand Prix by Ludovico Scarfiotti, without success.

77

77–78 The Honda, seen here during the trials for the Monaco Grand Prix, won only one race, the 1967 Italian Grand Prix, with John Surtees driving. This car, powerful and with a beautiful line, was over-heavy compared to the single-seaters against which it competed. The Honda had a 12-cylinder, 90 degree V engine, bore and stroke 78x52.2 mm, 2,994 cc, giving 400 hp at 12,000 rpm. The exhaust pipes were placed inside the V of the cylinders (as in the 1967 Ferrari and Brabham-Repco) and there were 6 gears. Surtees won the race with a record average speed of 226.119 kmph.

78

79

80

79 The world champion of 1962 and 1968, Graham Hill, in the Italian Grand Prix in which he suffered bad luck. Driving a Lotus-Ford he was well in the lead when he was forced to withdraw due to a technical fault. His team-mate, Jim Clark, who dropped a lap at the beginning of the race because of a puncture, managed to regain first place after a well-fought chase, but on the last lap he was delayed by a petrol leak and overtaken by Brabham and Surtees who were neck and neck down to the last metre.

80 Rear view of the Eagle Weslake. In most Formula I single-seaters of that period the bodywork covered only the front of the car, and the engine was completely open.

81 The Lotus-Climax in which Jim Clark drove in the 1967 Monaco Grand Prix.

82 The Ferrari Dino and P4 prototypes halted in front of the pits during practice for the 1967 Monza Thousand Kilometres.

83 Monaco in 1967: Louis Chiron, who was one of the greatest pre-war drivers, starts the Formula V race (single-seaters with Volkswagen engines) on the morning of the Monaco Grand Prix.

84 Enzo Ferrari at Monza with a P4 prototype. The famous builder from Modena is never present at a race, but, by long-standing tradition, always goes to the official trials when his cars compete at Monza.

85 Rear view of the 250 LM Ferrari, one of Maranello's most brilliant sports cars. It has a 60 degree V 12-cylinder engine of 2,953 cc at the rear. Its success on tracks throughout the world has made this model justly popular. It has been bought by private teams, and the one shown here is owned by an American racing association.

86

87

88

86 The Matra MS 11 Formula I driven by J.-P. Beltoise in the Italian Grand Prix at Monza in 1968. It had a V12 engine made in France, which did not give very good results. The Matra 12-cylinder engine was withdrawn from Formula I in 1969 to undergo a redesign as it was too heavy and cumbersome, and not lubricated in a satisfactory way. Nevertheless it was still used that year in endurance races, and reappeared in a new Formula I chassis in 1970.

87 Jackie Stewart dominated the 1969 season in a Matra powered by an 8-cylinder Ford engine. The chassis of the Matra MS 80 was entirely different from the previous year's MS 10. The weight distribution was carefully planned with the petrol tanks in the centre, giving a bulbous shape to the car. One can also see the first solution adopted by Matra after the abolition of the suspension-mounted airfoils to ensure the adhesion of the rear wheels.

88 The second version of the BMW Formula II with an ordinary cylinder head, still with four valves per cylinder, was designed with a monocoque chassis by the Englishman, Len Terry, and made by Dornier, the aeronautical manufacturers. Large airfoils were fitted on the BMW, like those on the Formula I cars. Of great technical quality, the BMW seen here, driven by Joseph Siffert, became one of the best cars of its class, even though it only succeeded in beating cars fitted with Cosworth Ford engines during its final (1970) season.

89 Using a British-made chassis, BMW made a Formula II in 1968 which had an unusual engine with a special cylinder-head, invented by Apfelbeck. It had four valves in radial formation, controlled by single cams. The results, however, were not satisfactory and this format was abandoned, even though approximately 240 hp had been confidently predicted.

89

90

90 A Porsche 910. Powered by a classical Porsche engine with an air cooling system the 910 sports model was produced in small numbers and sold to private drivers who obtained brilliant results with it. In 1967 it was the official team car, initially called Carrera 10 after the famous Carrera 6, but shorter and lighter. In 1967 and 1968, 8-cylinder engines of 2,200, 2,400 and 2,600 cc were also used. A Porsche 910 with an 8-cylinder, 2,200 cc engine, won the 1967 Targa Florio.

91 A Porsche 917; the most powerful car to compete in the longer races in 1969. It is unlike the previous racing Porsches in that its engine is made up of 12 cylinders facing one another with the drive gears placed in the centre. It is in fact made of two 911 R, 6-cylinder engines coupled together. Like all Porsche cars it has an air cooling system with two overhead camshafts; there is a Bosch indirect fuel injection system. The 917 develops 520 hp at 8,000 rpm. There are two types of bodywork, one short and one long, the latter being suitable for fast circuits. Speeds up to 350 kmph have been attained. Because of the length of the engine the driving position is very far forward which makes it more difficult for the driver. Although only twenty-five models have been made some are in private hands.

91

92

93

92–93 Two aspects of the Ford GT 40 in which Schlesser and Ligier took part in the 1967 1,000 Kilometres. This beautiful American car has a V8 rear engine of 5,023 cc giving 400 hp at 6,000 rpm, and weighs 1,100 kg. It has a maximum speed of 290 kmph. Schlesser and Ligier came sixth in the final results, but took first place in their category of sports cars over 2,000 cc.

94–95–96 The 1967 Ferrari Dino characterised by its rounded windscreen which completely covers the cockpit. At the back can be seen the 'rollbar' which has a stabilizing function.

97 World champion in 1967, the Ferrari P 4 obtained outstanding results in the Daytona 24 Hours and in the Monza 1,000 Kilometres, driven by two team pairs: Bandini-Amon and Parkes-Scarfiotti. It had different suspension and bodywork from the 1966 P 3 model, but retained the classical V12 engine of 4,000 cc. Its hp was increased to 440 at 8,000 rpm, thanks to the 3 valved cylinder heads copied from the Formula I engine. The Ferraris' five gears were new, as was the arrangement of the rear brakes on the wheels rather than on the gearbox output shaft, as in the P 3. Illustrated here is the coupé model, driven at Daytona by Parkes who came second to the Bandini-Amon Spyder.

94

97

98

99

98 (Previous page.) For the Can-Am (Canada-America)
series of races reserved for two-seater sports cars with no limit
to the cubic capacity, Ferrari prepared the 612 model, in which
the 6 stands for the cubic capacity (6,200 cc) and the 12 for the
number of cylinders. After a brief appearance at the end of 1968
the car was completely developed in 1969, with a relatively short
but penetrating body. It had a V12 engine of 6,200 cc, and in the
latest version developed 640 hp at 8,000 rpm. It had five Ferrari
gears with very wide wheel rims (14 inches).

99–100 The American 2 F Chaparral prototype is a highly
original car with a stabilizing flap which can be controlled by the
driver. The engine, which is placed at the rear, is a V8 Chevrolet
of 6,996 cc, bore and stroke 107.9x95.5 mm, giving 570 hp at
6,500 rpm, dry weight 830 kg, and a top speed of around
320 kmph. Another peculiarity of the Chaparral is that it has a
3 speed automatic gear box with a hydraulic gear change
mechanism. In spite of frequent mechanical faults this car gave
good results during the 1967 season, including the outright
victory at the Brands Hatch 500 Kilometres.

101 After having considerable success with cars of small cubic
capacity, Alpine Renault built a prototype of the 3,000 cc class,
with a V8 engine designed for them by Amedeo Gordini. These
cars, with different types of bodywork, held the road well and
were brilliantly streamlined.

102 Matra, the large French missile construction company,
began making racing cars after the take-over of Bonnet which
was partly financed by them. Having built small Formula III
and Formula II single-seaters, Matra decided to venture into the
Formula I and prototype bracket. The first Matra prototype did
extremely well in the 24 Hours at Le Mans in 1968, and the
following year the company built the 630 model, shown here,
which made its debut in the 1,000 Kilometres at Monza. Its
performance was brilliant at Le Mans but it had little success due
to a few minor inconveniences. Matra continue to make the same
type of car with V12 Matra engines, developing over 400 hp.

100

56

101

102

103 The Alfa Romeo 33, a two-litre sports car with a V8 engine and fuel injection, giving 250 hp. Extremely fast, stable and easy to handle, this car has already won some brilliant victories, especially in hill races. Without the trouble caused by its original front suspension, it would have won many more. The 33 came out in 1967 in a coupé version with very good lines.

104 The Alfa Romeo 33-3, while keeping certain structural points of the two-litre 33, was an entirely new car which made its first appearance in the Sebring Twelve Hours in 1969, although it had little hope of being placed. The overall perfecting of the car, which took place in the following months, gave excellent results, and it did very well in July of that year. The first victory of this V8 engine of 3,000 cc was won by Andrea de Adamich at the inaugural event of the Austrian circuit at Zeltweg. It is characterised by the highly original streamlining solution with the two radiators on either side of the cockpit. It develops 400 hp at 9,000 rpm.

05 The Mk IV Ford, winner of the 24 Hours at Le Mans in 1967 after a long battle with the Ferraris. The building of this car was supervised by Carroll Shelby, and large sums were spent on it. It has an 8-cylinder, 90 degrees V engine at the rear, 6,980 cc, bore and stroke 107.7x96 mm, compression ratio of 10.75, giving 530 hp at 6,200 rpm. The Le Mans victory was won by a team consisting of Dan Gurney and A. J. Foyt (the latter had previously won the Indianapolis 500 three times). They had a record average speed of 218.038 kmph.

106 New Zealander Denis Hulme in the McLaren M8D sports-racing car with which he became Can-Am Champion for the second time. McLaren cars won 31 of the 39 races during the first five years of the Canadian-American Challenge Cup series. The M8D was powered by a 7½-litre Chevrolet engine based on the Corvette 430 ZL-1 cylinder block and producing about 675 horsepower. The engine, prepared at McLaren's engine facility near Detroit, drove the rear wheels through a Hewland LG600 four-speed transaxle.

107 The Swedish driver Reine Wisell, a member of Gold Leaf Team Lotus, driving the Cosworth Ford-engined Lotus 72, identical to the car with which the late Jochen Rindt won the drivers' world championship in 1970. The wedge-shaped nose and side-mounted radiators have since been copied by other racing car manufacturers. The V8 3-litre engine, of 440 horsepower, drives the Lotus through a five-speed Hewland transaxle. The front and rear airfoils are the subject of strict regulations regarding their size and location.

108 1970 world champion Jochen Rindt. The 28-years old Austrian driver crashed and died while practising for the 1970 Italian Grand Prix at Monza, and did not then know that he was world champion. It was not until a month after his death that the results of the US Grand Prix showed for certain that no other driver could score as many points as Rindt. He was sponsored by Ford of Austria in 1962, and made his first important win at the Crystal Palace, London, in 1964. He remained in England, driving for Cooper, and was a winner at Le Mans in 1965. In December 1968 he joined the Lotus team.

109 The Matra-Simca MS670 which in 1972, in the hands of Graham Hill and Henri Pescarolo, gave France her first Le Mans victory since 1950. Powered by a 450 horsepower V12 engine similar to Matra's Formula I power unit, and using a five-speed ZF transmission, the MS670 was tried at Le Mans with both long and short-tail bodywork. The short-tailed winning car, which averaged over 121 mph for the 24 hours, including pit stops, finished 10 laps ahead of the long-tailed MS670 of Francois Cevert and Howden Ganley.

08

109

10 Denny Hulme practising his Yardley McLaren-Ford M19A for the 72 Monaco Grand Prix. The McLarens of Hulme (who had already won that ar's South African Grand Prix) and his American team-mate, Peter Revson, hieved the most impressive reliability record of any Formula I team in 1972. he tall air intake behind the driver's head is positioned so as to draw in a nooth flow of 'clean' air without disturbing the car's aerodynamic stability.

11 In the black and gold livery of its sponsors, the Ford-powered John ayer Special of 1972 was in fact a refined version of the previous season's tus 72D. The combination of Emerson Fittipaldi (seen here practising for e Monaco Grand Prix) and three years of development on a brilliant initial sign was to prove unbeatable. The use of torsion bar suspension and

inboard brakes helped to make the car particularly competitive when braking for or accelerating from corners. The JPS was powered by the Ford DFV V8 engine, which already has over 50 GP successes to its credit.

112 Jackie Stewart at Brands Hatch, driving his Tyrrell-Ford 003, the car which earned him the 1971 world championship. Designed and built at the Tyrrell headquarters in Surrey by Derek Gardner and his staff, the Tyrrell-Ford was planned on the basis of 'sophisticated orthodoxy', using straightforward design principles with meticulous attention to detail. The bulbous body amidships was reminiscent of the Matra-Simca MS80 with which Stewart had gained the 1969 title. The Tyrrell-Ford 003 continued to be used for much of the 1972 season pending the development of its successor, the 005.

SOME POST-WAR DRIVERS: Alberto Ascari, killed at Monza in 1955. He was twice world champion for Ferrari, in 1952 and 1953.

Juan Manual Fangio, the Argentinian who is the only driver in the world to have won five world titles, four of them in successive years.

Stirling Moss, although one of the greatest post-war drivers, never succeeded in winning the world championship.

Phil Hill gave up racing driving in the mid-sixties. In 1961, driving a Ferrari, he won the world title.

Graham Hill won the world championship twice; in a BRM in 1962 and in a Lotus in 1968.

Already many times world champion of motorcycle racing, John Surtees won the racing driving title in 1964 while at the wheel of a Ferrari.

Jack Brabham also builds racing cars. He won the world title in 1959 and in 1960 while driving a Cooper, and again in 1966 in his own Brabham.

Jim Clark, who was killed in 1968, was acclaimed as the best all-round racing driver of his time. He won the world title in 1963 and 1965 in a Lotus.

Lorenzo Bandini, the great Italian champion of the Ferrari team, was killed in 1967 towards the end of the Grand Prix at Monaco.

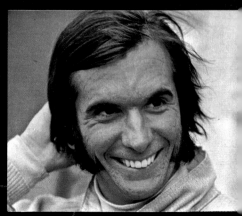

Driving a Brabham, the New Zealander Denis Hulme won the world championship in 1967.

Jackie Stewart of Scotland, who was world champion in 1969, won fame at the wheel of a Matra-Ford.

1972 world champion Emerson Fittipaldi of Brazil at 25 years of age the youngest driver ever to win motor racing's top award.